Design
Is in the
Details

Design
Is in the
Details

Decorating Indoors & Out

Brad Mee

Sterling Publishing Co., Inc. New York
A Sterling/Chapelle Book

Chapelle Limited

Owner: Jo Packham

Editor: Karmen Potts Quinney

Cover: Photography by Dino Tonn Photography
Interior Design by David Michael Miller Associates

If you have any questions or comments, please contact:
Chapelle Ltd., Inc., P.O. Box 9252 Ogden, UT 84409
(801) 621-2777 • FAX (801) 621-2788
• e-mail: chapelle@ chapelleltd.com
• website: www.chapelleltd.com

Library of Congress Cataloging-in-Publication Data Available

Mee,Brad.
    Design is in the details: decorating indoors & out / Brad Mee.
        p. cm.
    Includes index.
    ISBN 0-8069-3019-5
        1. Interior decoration. 2. Garden ornaments and furniture. I. Title.

    NK 1980 .M 44 2001

    747--dc21

10 9 8 7 6 5 4 3 2 1   2001020624

Published by Sterling Publishing Company, Inc.,
387 Park Avenue South, New York, NY 10016
© 2001 by Brad Mee
Distributed in Canada by Sterling Publishing
℅ Canadian Manda Group, One Atlantic Avenue, Suite 105
Toronto, Ontario, Canada M6K 3E7
Distributed in Great Britain and Europe by Chris Lloyd at Orca Book
Services, Stanley House, Fleets Lane, Poole BH15 3AJ, England.
Distributed in Australia by Capricorn Link (Australia) Pty. Ltd.
P.O. Box 704, Windsor, NSW 2756 Australia
Printed in China
All Rights Reserved

Sterling ISBN 0-8069-3019-5

Introduction 9

CONTENTS

INTRODUCTION

In the design of a home and its landscape, nothing is truer than the statement, "the design is in the details." Details are the finishing touches, the elements of style that bring uniqueness and intrigue to a space . . . be it a beautiful room or an inviting garden. They, more than any other part of the design, reflect the individuality and personal style of those who live in and enjoy a home.

The need to embellish our homes can be traced back as far as our origins. Ancient caves boast painted wall murals, prehistoric pottery is displayed and decorated with pattern and color. Then, as now, the living space became "detailed" in part, to enhance the experience and to express the personality, life-style, and taste of its inhabitants. This seemingly instinctual desire to adorn and stylize our homes is as strong now as ever.

Once the decision determining both the desired feel and the intended purpose of the space is made, detail takes hold. A direction is set and the imagination cut loose. But where does detail exist? Simple. It exists wherever an appreciative eye stops, lingers, and admires. It is found in countless forms—the texture of the walls, the patterns in the flooring, the colors of the ceiling, the characteristics of the furnishings, the accents in architecture, and the infinite collectibles and objects proudly showcased throughout the home and garden. Just as an accessory is defined as something extra or complementary, so it is with details. Details are the accessories that complement and complete a space.

Beyond personal expression, detail performs a number of roles. Detail orchestrates the visual experience by creating focal points and points of interest. By introducing a flavor of other lands, it can transport us to another time or place, if only in our imaginations. It induces emotion. In total, it transforms the basic shell of an uninspired home and landscape to a setting that excites the senses and imagination in a unique and personal way.

The method of bringing character to your design with detail depends, in a large part, on your personal taste, whether it is minimalist contemporary, time-honored traditional, comfortably casual, or simply eclectic. There is no exact science nor are there hard-and-fast rules to "detailing" your home, but there are basic qualities that can act as guides. Compatibility to the décor, the consideration of period style, the display of color, an attention to size and scale, the use of textures and materials, and a regard to positioning, all come into play. With these directives in mind, incorporating details that you love will help you create the home of your dreams.

As you explore the following pages, you will discover ideas that will help you identify and savor the many ways details are innovatively used to create memorable, personal spaces. From an enchanting room to an irresistible garden, these scenes will inspire you to express your style through the magic that details can bring to your home.

In theatre, the walls, floors, and ceilings are the backdrop for the drama. In your home, these surfaces can actually create the drama. Both literally and figuratively, these surfaces provide an expansive opportunity to express your personal style and taste. Walls are, after all, the largest surface in your home. Ceilings and floors are not far behind. They are structurally important as they provide a roof over your head and shelter from the storm. As empty canvases, their design significance is equally important as these planes of space set the stage for the remaining aspects of your design scheme.

The mood of a space can be directed through the creative "detailing" of surfaces. The textures, the colors, the patterns, the materials, all influence their character. In addition, surfaces are important as they invite display of other design components. Walls, for instance, provide the setting for art, architectural accents, mirrors, and, in reality, perform as the backdrop for windows and doors. Floors display rugs, furniture, and any other elements enhanced by this underfoot surface. The ceiling overhead rewards the upward-looking optimist with decorative light fixtures, structural beams, shapely moldings, and skylights.

As theatre is limited only by one's imagination, so is the detailing of surfaces. Settle in the middle of a room and examine the surfaces that surround you. Recognize the purpose of the space and determine the feel you would like it to express. Then let your creativity flow as you explore infinite ways to make your home's surfaces extraordinary.

SURFACES

Atmosphere. Ambiance. Mood. Whatever you want to call it, the walls in your home are enormously important in helping you create the "feel" you would like the space to express. Like huge blank canvases, walls welcome your ingenuity and personal expression of style.

Walls tempt detail as the desire to surround with texture, color, and infinite patterns and surface elements comes alive. Because walls, by sheer square footage, are the most sizable surface in the home, the effect of detail is powerful. They truly set the tone of the room. Wall finishes seem endless as paint, wall-

WALLS

paper, fabric, paneling, mirrors, and many accents and ornaments become options. Beyond the more obvious surface interests, walls are also detailed by stylized functional elements including doors, windows, vents, and fireplaces, to name a few. These, too, lend themselves to creative and individualized design.

I have a predilection for painting that lends joyousness to a wall.

Pierre Auguste Renoir

Nothing transforms the feel of a room more dramatically than a "redressing" of the walls. Whether through color, pattern, or texture, a freshly finished wall can set the tone of the room with new life and interest.

Color is the most common way to decorate the surface of interior walls and is also the most critical. Beyond creating an immediate mood, it can actually transform the way the room is perceived spatially. With a choice of infinite shades, the selection of color for your rooms should be based on your personal preferences as well as the properties of the space. The amount of light, the size, and the determined use of the room will effect how a color translates in your room. Do you want the room to be calming or exciting? Does the spatial quality of the room require special attention? Are there other design elements or details, such as furnishings, art, or accessories, whose color will influence your choice for the walls? Further, will a surface interest in the form of wallpaper, textures, or imagery help create the desired mood of the space? These are questions to be considered. In color, deep, rich jewel tones produce an intimate, romantic feel to a space. Golden-tinged shades and patinas lend a mellowed, rich ambiance from the old world of centuries past. The calmness of muted pastels is relaxing, while the drama of pure white can bring a fresh, edited look to a room. Whichever way you choose to detail this surface, be true to your personal taste and remember, just as you change, so can your walls. Nothing is set in stone.

PAGE 12
Brilliant purple and golden yellow walls energize this angular master bedroom suite. Peppered with glass block, the curved purple wall surrounds the shower stall and frames the bathroom's entry.

PAGE 13
Plaster walls are hand-finished with running layers of a taupe wash to create the look of century-old monastery walls. The result is dramatic without being jarring.

OPPOSITE

This bedroom's walls were completely covered with a hand-painted harlequin pattern in varying shades of beige and taupe. The darker diamonds were sponged over the lighter background to achieve the patterned effect.

UPPER RIGHT

Original 1926 tiles in shades of mint and black encase this small bathroom. The walls above the tile are painted to match the tilework. An enlarged border at the ceiling mimics the smaller running border in the tile while creating vertical height by drawing the eye upward.

UPPER LEFT

The walls of this playful powder room are covered with clouded-sky wallpaper as the perfect backdrop for the off-shaped mirror and abstract sculptures displayed. This treatment makes the small space seem larger as the walls have a sense of dimension and their boundaries seem lost in the sky.

LEFT

Crayon-colored walls are painted and patterned to appear sun-washed and weathered on this festive patio. The large space of gray plaster gives the effect of chipping fresco, further enhancing the arresting surface. A running horizontal border makes the entire wall appear wider.

It can be said that of all the surfaces in the home, you have the greatest "connection" with the floor. With every step you take, you are in direct contact with it. It silently calls to your senses—to the touch in texture and temperature, to sight in color and depth, and in sound it absorbs or reflects. Mostly, it calls to your imagination. What face do you want to put on this surface? As the floor is the foundation for both the physical structure and the personality of the room, it is best to determine the design and detail of this underfoot entity from the beginning of the creative process. Consider all the possibilities

FLOORS

. . . stone, brick, wood, tile, carpeting, rugs, and numerous others. Several questions need to be answered before making flooring decisions. What is the function of the room? What kind of wear will the floor experience? Will sound be a consideration? After all, floors perform a utilitarian function that should be the primary consideration. Once practicality is addressed, however, the detail process presents itself and the possibilities are unlimited.

Consider your floors as underfoot walls upon which you display your furnishings. For an understated backdrop that subtly supports your décor, consider plain or gently patterned surfaces such as carpeting, wooden flooring, or stone. To add drama or to frame groupings of furnishings within a room, beautifully patterned rugs, richly textured carpets, bold tiles, or a combination of dramatically contrasting elements is effective.

PAGE 16
Light wooden floors and a lushly textured rug are the perfect setting for this casually elegant room. The generously scaled upholstery, iron-based cocktail table, and warm wooden accent chairs are all richly finished in color and texture to reflect the strength of the selected flooring.

Tile has become one of the most popular flooring choices in the home. From deeply shaded slate and stone to the subtly toned marble and smoothly surfaced ceramics, tile offers wonderful opportunities to detail the floors of any room. Ceramic tile is nearly six thousand years old, dating back to a time when Egyptians formed tiles from clay in wooden frames. Since then, ceramics have been used throughout time and around the world to create culturally identifiable designs and motifs employing color, shapes, and patterns. From the brilliance of Moorish tiles in the Alhambra to the artistry of inlaid mosaics of ancient Roman's Herculaneum, tilework has been copied and interpreted in modern-day homes everywhere.

Beyond the use of tile as a primarily decorative medium, it also can effect the feel of a room spatially. Medium to large tiles on the floor of a smaller room can make it appear larger. Setting tiles on the diagonal or using a variety of sizes in the same space can give the room added dimension. The ability of tile to add detail in the form of color, texture, and pattern makes it a wonderful choice when determining the treatment of the floor.

OPPOSITE
In this dramatically detailed kitchen, the character begins with the brilliantly colored tiles designed and painted to look like a fringed Turkish rug.

LEFT
Suffused with color and detail, this tile-laden bathroom boasts Moroccan motifs that lead from the bordered ceramic floor, up the multiple-bordered walls, to the hand-finished burnished-gold walls. The distinctive towel hook and light fixture further the desired look.

19

Detailed flooring highlights the inspired interiors of these rooms as it sets the stage for the remaining elements of design.

RIGHT
Natural sisal enhances the tropical colors and relaxed furnishings of this casual sitting room.

BOTTOM RIGHT
A dramatic focal point is conceived with this elegantly inlaid-marble starburst centered in the gleaming wooden floor. A wonderful example of combining handsome yet ordinary flooring to create a look that is extraordinary.

BOTTOM LEFT
Continued from the outside into the main living room, chiseled stone tiles surround a rustic inlaid-wood floor partially covered with a timeworn Persian rug.

OPPOSITE
In a room surrounded by glass, a custom-designed rug brings the focus to the floor and gives structure to a sparse furniture grouping.

The overhead canopy of a room—the ceiling—by actual height, helps determine and define the room's overall scale, size, and proportions. In many ways, it directs the physical reaction to the space. Historically, ceilings have been held in "high" esteem as they were constructed to soar far above the floor with decorated, distinctive, imaginative details. Today, low, unadorned ceilings are more prevalent and are considered finished when simply covered with white paint. Sometimes this

CEILINGS

treatment is advisable as it offers relief from other design elements in the room. However, the ability to add character and a unique quality to your living space by adding detail to a ceiling should never be overlooked. Consider the possibilities . . . hand-painted designs, trompe l'oeil artistry, an expanse of color, paneling, vaulting, and beams, to name a few. Furthermore, moldings, cornices, and stenciled borders can be used to connect the walls to the ceiling and draw the eyes upward. Perhaps the best inspiration to add detail to a ceiling is to take the lead from nature. As you look up toward the sky, recognize the impressive scene above. Why not create one in your home?

Lying in bed would be an altogether perfect and supreme experience if only one had a coloured pencil long enough to draw on the ceiling.

G. K. Chesterton

The options for ceiling detail range from the simplest of finishes and fixtures to the most elaborate of beams, iron, and imagery. For some rooms, simply darkening a ceiling to make it appear lower, or lightening it to make it recede skywards, is detail enough. Other rooms boast awe-inspiring lighting effects, hand-painted scenes, or an artistry of architectural beams and plasterwork. As with other surfaces, the key is to determine the desired mood of the space and to address the treatment of the ceiling from there. Because the norm is the un-remarkable treatment of white paint, your endeavors to detail the ceiling have nowhere to go but up!

PAGE 22
Hand-worked iron lends a regional charm to the rustic beams of this grand ceiling.

PAGE 23
An uncluttered gallery hall is framed above by soaring plastered rafters. The line of the rafters is continued to the outdoor patio and is accented with violet sun-breaking sails. Notice the overall grid is continued in the outdoor wall and the indoor window frames.

OPPOSITE
Formerly a white-walled breezeway, this solarium boasts a hand-painted classical compass design from which an antique iron chandelier is hung. The walls, too, are hand-painted to replicate stone.

UPPER LEFT
Crackled-glass panels and hanging spotlights are dramatically suspended above the dining area of this material-rich home. The glass sensationally filters and spreads the downcast light from inset cans in the ceiling surface.

BOTTOM LEFT
In this magnificent billiard room, the trilevel ceiling is detailed with elaborately painted borders and beautifully finished surfaces in pond green and burnished orange. Creative use of lighting not only illuminates the table below but up-lights the head-turning treatment above.

The floors, walls, and ceilings are a structure's basic components. "Fixed Assets" are added to the structure and are a home's permanent

elements that are functionally essential. These assets—doors, windows, staircases, fireplaces, sinks, bathtubs—are all considered part of the "bones" of a home, yet, in reality, are the flesh that gives the structure a persona all its own. Among their functions, they dutifully provide protection from the outdoors, natural light for the indoors, access from floor to floor, warmth, and waterworks. By enriching them with detail, these utilitarian elements play an important part in defining the personality and character of the home.

FIXED ASSETS

If a home offered a one-man show, the door would play the lead. It is multitalented, multidimensional, and multifunctional. In the home, the door does it all. Functionally,

the door is the sentinel of the space. It provides security and protection from the intrusion of drafts, unwanted light and sounds, and, of course, uninvited visitors. On the other hand, it acts as the entrance, welcoming while, at the same time, hinting at the style of the interior through its own design and detail. In the interior, doors direct movement throughout the home and provide transition from one room or space to another. Doors can become effective focal points in a room. And just as costumes add character to the actor, so does detail to the door. Wood, glass, metal, and mirrors

DOORS

are just a few of the materials used to create interesting doors. Curved, arched, paneled, paired, folding, swinging, louvered, and pocket are just a few of their many forms. Colors, patterns, and surface treatments wardrobe the door while endless choices in hardware and decorative accessories act as jewelry. By characterizing the door in this way, this most basic, yet most talented of the home's assets offers itself to applause and ovations as it is brought to its decorative potential through detail.

Literally, a door is two sided . . . so is its appeal in the home. First, as a necessity, it secures a space and presents a passageway. Second, it offers itself creatively to detail and decorative design. Perhaps no other architectural element has been so innovatively transformed to take advantage of both the functional and decorative opportunities available to it as has the door.

PAGE 28
Double-studded iron doors offer a hint of the handsome courtyard beyond. Once inside, another set of substantial, carved doors becomes the focal point of the entry, as framed by a scattering of enormous pots and effective mood lighting.

PAGE 29
Hardware and detail can convert even the simplest of doors to the most intriguing. A distinctive personality is cast upon this single arched door with the addition of bold carvings, solid iron handle, and alluring window grate.

PAGES 30–31
Designed to both shield and reveal, glass-paned doors offer enlightened ways to bring person-ality to an interior. Why only consider solid wooden doors inside? Stained, leaded, and etched glass offer both light and privacy. Clear glass panels present a barrier to sound while keeping the space open to light and sight beyond the door.

RIGHT
Etched glass customizes this door, repeating the dramatic angles of the ceiling's beams.

OPPOSITE
Like a work of art, these stunning double doors act as an unforgettable backdrop to the mosaic-topped stone entry table of this timeless foyer.

Nothing is quite so instinctual as our attraction to fire—the warmth, the aroma, the mesmerizing flicker and glow of the flames. While we no longer rely on the power of fire for our daily existence, like cave dwellers of ages past, we have created a permanent place in our homes for fire. As a result, the fireplace has become one of the most popular features in today's living areas. As a design element, it is one of the most important. In fact, so strong is the appeal of the fireplace that in some rooms, a mantelpiece is used to detail a blank wall just to create the illusion of an existing fireplace.

FIREPLACES

The two most critical criteria in determining the appearance of the fireplace are the character and the size of the room in which it is placed. Compatibility with the design character of the room, whether it is Victorian or contemporary, should directly influence the detail of the fireplace. The mantelpiece, the hearth, the surround, the grate, and the fire irons all need to be consistent with the other design elements of the space.

Similarly, the scale of the fireplace should be harmoniously proportionate to the size of the room. If it is too large, like a bully it will overwhelm the space. If the scale needs to minimized, the detail used to decorate the fireplace should be minimal and colored so as to blend with the walls of the room. On the other hand, if the existing fireplace is too small, it will appear insufficient as an important decorative feature. Expanding and decorating the fire surround or adding color to the bordering wall gives the look of a larger fireplace that will help divert the eye from a diminutive opening.

A sitting room without a fireplace can appear lost, lacking a center of gravity as well as a welcoming, warming feature. As a focal point, fireplaces are unequalled. They create a natural, interesting design element—one open to creative detail—on which the eye can rest. Some boast broad-shouldered mantles, offering the perfect location for displaying art and accessories. Others present a plain front structure to be covered with strong, architectural detail and materials. Still others, in an effort to emphasize the architectural lines and form of the fireplace, are purposefully left unadorned. These decisions to detail a fireplace are truly significant as they become part of the most visual and comforting features of the home.

PAGE 35
Understated and elegant, the broad opening of this fireplace gives a sense of width to the refined room. The clean molding keeps the fixture from being overbearing and allows the fireplace to join rather than conflict with the nearby artwork. Together, they become the room's most significant focal point.

RIGHT
Covered in stainless steel, this sculptured fireplace floats in the middle of the main living area, becoming a point of interest from all areas of the room.

The "keeper of the flame"—the fireplace—is all about presentation. Fireplaces come in endless forms and their style should be in keeping with the setting in which they are placed. The fireplace on the upper left of the opposite page becomes the base of a multitiered metal sculpture that soars above the room. Clean, curved lines captured in polished wood in the photograph on the upper right give this fireplace a comfortable, contemporary feel. The elaborately carved wooden fireplace on the bottom right becomes a work of art and is capped with a coordinating mirror, completing the perfect focal point for this classic hacienda living room. The fireplace on the bottom left combines brick and stone to create a refined, masculine fireplace with handsome patterns and a lion-head crown.

As host to some of the most memorable times spent with family and friends, the outdoor living space has become one of the most popular settings for a fireplace. After all, didn't we all start our love affair with fire outdoors, roasting marshmallows over a pit of crackling flames?

There are many ways to create a fireplace in your landscape. Some nestle in the corners of an outdoor patio or terrace. Others become part of the actual structure of the home and take on the characteristics of the exterior walls. More simply, iron bowls on stands become mobile firepits and can be placed anywhere in the yard where there is open sky above and plenty of gathering room around the fire. Of course, more primitive, but equally as enjoyable, is a permanent firepit dug and formed into the ground. Whichever way you choose to house fire in your outdoor living space, you are guaranteed to be creating an alluring place to gather and enjoy the charm of fire.

UPPER RIGHT
Standing on its own, this large outdoor fireplace is positioned on the rear of the terraced patio and draws the party to the heat of its flames as well as the view of the surrounding desert.

BOTTOM RIGHT
A welcoming sight on a cool crisp day, this flagstone-faced fireplace invites quiet reading and a place to warm up after a swim in the adjacent pool.

OPPOSITE
As flames take the chill from the desert night, a crackling fire in this enchanting patio sets the stage for a quiet evening outdoors.

Even before a staircase is "detailed," it adds considerable character to a space. By its mere existence, it suggests movement within the home. More intriguingly, it produces the mystery of what lies beyond—at either the top or bottom of the stairs. Curiosity comes alive with a glimpse of these areas from the far end of the steps. By accentuating these areas with detail in the form of color, texture, lighting, or accessories, this curiosity is fueled.

Staircases are a dramatic pairing of form and function. Functionally, they should be designed to safely and comfortably provide access to other levels in a space. In their form, detail can flourish. The assorted elements—the baluster, the handrail, the riser, and the tread—all offer expression of personal style. The baluster exists to support the handrail and to create a

STAIRCASES

sense of enclosure for an open staircase. To it, creative detail is imaginatively applied with stone, wood, glass, and even guidewires as eye-catching accents to the staircase. Handrails of carved wood, polished metal, twisted iron, and even wire and rope lend a hand to those who ascend and descend the staircase. The risers and treads, while underfoot, boast a variety of elements—stone, wood, concrete, and metal. Some are covered with runners, carpeting, or tile. Others are hand-painted to create the illusion of a Persian carpet or to repeat a color or design present elsewhere in the room. Creatively, different materials can be used on the risers and tread of the same staircase to add dimension and interest.

Attention to the lighting and color used on and around a staircase is important. They affect the sense of openness as well as the ability to visually judge the steps while walking up or down. Detailing the walls with paint treatments or displays of art and photography also adds to this architectural feature and presents a wonderful opportunity to express your personal style.

The staircase should be thought of as a functional sculpture. Like art, it captures the eye with the movement of its lines and curves. Steps may be like solid blocks or, alternatively, staggered slabs supported in midair. Handrails take on personality as serpentine twists or simple geometric lines stretching from the base to the top of the structure. The balusters may conceal or reveal the steps, depending on the design and materials that form them. Even enclosed staircases can attract when detail is added to bring points of interest and intrigue. Color, displays of wall art, and unusual use of materials as the basic structural elements of the staircase can help it become a centerpiece of style in the home.

PAGE 41
Sometimes the staircase is the only place in a home with enough wall area to display large art. Here, the hand-forged iron baluster complements the sculptural and architectural quality of the art.

RIGHT
Mosaic-inlaid risers and contrasting stone treads give this staircase an old-world look, alive with the detailed work of talented artisans.

OPPOSITE
A conventional, partially enclosed staircase features an imaginative handrail of chain ascending the wall. In the interest of safety, it is effective. In the interest of character, it is outstanding.

LEFT
Sleek and sophisticated, this stainless steel spiral staircase entices one to ascend the steps to see what exists above. The plain, curved walls and decorative lighting highlight the twisting structure like a work of art.

OPPOSITE
Stainless steel stairway rails sweep fluidly up the height of this glowing entry. Note the creative guide wires that enclose the stairway space. Standing at attention, a brightly colored column enhances the brilliant walls and slate floors.

In ancient Rome, the ideal place to relax and luxuriate was the thermae, or baths. The effect of water on the body and spirit made these public facilities an escape from the toil and stress of everyday life. Today's private bath is the thermae of the home. And now, as then, this room encourages the shutting away of the world and surrendering to the revitalizing and therapeutic nature of water and all it represents—long, private soaks, invigorating showers, relaxing steam, and the aroma of natural herbal soaps. The essence of this private oasis is created by the physical nature of the space. Tile, stone, marble, mosaics, and mirrors dress the surfaces of today's bathrooms and powder

BATHS

rooms. Imaginative takes on traditional fixtures come alive in spacious showers, dramatic tubs, and distinctive sinks floating on glass counters above exposed plumbing. From eye-catching backgrounds to handcrafted hardware, luxurious towels, accessories and furnishings, all add to the experience of what, not long ago, was a small uninviting room designed purely for function. Today's bathroom has evolved into a feast for the senses and a showcase of detail.

47

Because the master bath is a private space that is not often visited by guests, it welcomes an even more personal sense of style that is uniquely yours. To many, the bath is a well-earned escape at the end of the day and should reflect this with its amenities. Soft towels, adjustable lighting, aromatic potpourris, candles, herbal soaps, and a "do not disturb" sign hung on the door is all you need to lose yourself in this luxurious, albeit temporary, retreat.

There are many ways to bring a sense of luxury to a bathroom. The simplest is to stock it with thickly absorbent towels that wrap you in comfort when used. Wall sconces create an ambiance that overhead lighting cannot provide. Adding a dimmer switch will allow you to adjust the amount of light desired. Bring in the unexpected. A polished French buffet serves wonderfully as a vanity. Employ a unique sink for an artsy, eclectic look. Welcome natural light wherever possible and use glass block, etched, or stained glass if needed for privacy. Swatches of fabric can soften the hard edge of some bathrooms. Drape the windows and create canopies overhead to take advantage of the decorative quality that luxurious fabrics can give. Replace characterless synthetic surfaces with stone, tile, or mosaics. If there is room, be daring and welcome a chaise or relaxing chair for comfort. Think of the bath as your personal haven and invite detail that makes it distinctively yours.

PAGE 46
Completely filled with detail, this spectacular bathroom space is inspired by an antique Russian zinc tub filled from the spouting mouth of the wall-framed lion. Elaborately tiled surfaces and an orchestra of iron candlesticks add to the character of this truly distinctive bath.

LEFT
Brilliant color, rich textures, and head-turning detail add drama and interest to this small bath.

OPPOSITE
With luxury as a guide, this bath was designed around the sumptuous canopied tub favored with its own iron chandelier. Soft putty tones, flickering candles, and sparkling glass block add to the ambiance. Note the open shower located behind the enclosed tub.

Sometimes the best things come in small packages. That certainly holds true for today's powder room. By its very nature—small and experienced in brief periods—it invites over-the-top detail that delights all who enter. It is the perfect stage for creating theatre using color, glass, tile, stone, and distinctive finishes on the walls and ceilings.

Look beyond the conventional ways to light this space and feel free to introduce unique character with distinctive accessories and ornaments.

The area of the home that truly deserves the title of the living room is, in most cases, the kitchen. No longer a utilitarian workplace designed solely for cooking, the kitchen has become the heart of the home. Its role extends far beyond food preparation. It serves as a gathering place for family and friends. We dine in it, entertain in it, store food and cookware in it, do homework in it, pay bills in it, and house the majority of the home's appliances in it. It is the room in which we live.

KITCHENS

Unlike the sterile, stainless steel kitchens popular in the past decade, today's kitchen incorporates details that reflect and enhance the way we live in and use this multifunctional space. Natural materials, creative lighting, task stations, and unique furnishings are included to help create a welcoming room that invites day-to-day living as well as casual entertaining.

Once the layout of a kitchen is established—one that promotes efficiency and comfort with the cooking function—the personality of the space can be created. Cooking is an art. Why not develop a "studio" that encourages the creativity and adventure cooking can entail?

Whether creating a new kitchen, reconstructing an old one, or just lending a fresh, new look to an existing space, the options are endless. To start, consider the surfaces. Would the room benefit from color and texture on the walls? Fans or moldings on the ceiling? Tile, wood, stone, or rugs on the floor? Consider the numerous options for countertop surfaces that promise to make a big difference in a kitchen's appearance. Easy changes that can also transform the space include new panels to face appliances, refinishing or replacing door fronts for cabinetry or simply changing out the hardware used throughout the room. Add a few glass cabinet door fronts to display favorite dinnerware for all to see, or add beams or hooks to the ceiling and hang copper pots and dried herbs within reach. The current trend moves away from wall-hugging, built-in cabinetry toward incorporating free-floating working islands and freestanding furnishings, suggesting the introduction of Grandmother's hutch, country table, or sideboard to add warmth and timelessness to the room. Hutches, desks, or existing cabinets can house the family's computer for all to enjoy. Ultimately, the best kitchen is one that facilitates the many ways it is used while providing warmth and comfort at the same time. The details added can help accomplish both.

With so much time spent in the kitchen, it is important that the room is comfortable and reflects your personal taste. Detail is added to the basics—the working, functional appliances and equipment of the space. From this point forward, personal style and detail dictate the direction of the design.

PAGE 52
A commercial-style kitchen captures a touch of whimsy as high-wire sculptures perform below a faux painted sky, providing light for this working, yet comfortable, room.

PAGES 54–55
Like your grandmother's kitchen, this room evokes a sense of comfort through its simplicity in detail and display. Undressed sash windows and glass-front cabinets welcome a soft light that shines through colored-glass collectibles peering over a view of the outdoors.

OPPOSITE
Saturated with character, this playful kitchen treats every surface as an opportunity to entertain with detail. A flying pig leaps a cabinet masquerading as the Chrysler building. Flagstone countertops are home to an assortment of quirky animals as color lands on decorative pots, plates, and urns throughout this frivolous, yet fully functional space.

UPPER RIGHT
This kitchen draws its strength from architectural detail and a restrained yet powerful use of color and shape. By facing the appliances and cabinets with matching maple, these functioning aspects of the kitchen become a warm backdrop for the more artistic details of the room.

BOTTOM RIGHT
Spare and sophisticated, this step-up kitchen is alive with understated detail. Creativity illuminates as running lights surround the base of the room and overhead halogens hang freely over the kitchen island. Contemporary glassware is displayed on glass shelves to allow the lighting to catch their every detail.

SHOWING OFF

The walls are finished, the floors are polished, and the furniture is placed. Yet, something is missing. That something is the accessories. They bring life to a room. Just as jewelry is lastly added to adorn a beautifully gowned woman, accessories are the finishing touches applied to a well-dressed room. They complete it. Accessories can be found at every turn—the framed pieces on the walls, the decorative pillows on the sofa, the collectibles on the shelves, and the vase, lamp, and books gathered on the chest. The list seems endless. Yet, among these infinite items is the common thread that they, more than any other element of detail or design, reveal the unique taste and style of those who live in the space.

The accessories with the most impact are those that tell a story or make a head-turning statement. Items selected merely to "go with the room" end up being bland and unremarkable in comparison. Be bold in your choices and display the things you love—treasured items, photographs, and keepsakes rich in expression and experiences. They tell your story of interests, values, travels, and the people and places you cherish. Even the simple characteristics of accessories, whether a crystal vase, a textured earthen jug, or a ceramic lamp, speak volumes of the style and taste of their

The home should be the treasure chest of living.

Le Corbusier

owner. The artistry of displaying these pieces can add further impact to their placement in the home. Some people prefer an orderly, minimalistic look, while others prefer organized clutter. Either way, the choice and display of the pieces is a form of art—one practiced through adding and subtracting, resulting in the perfect arrangement. Whether standing alone or grouped in eye-catching collections, accessories with unique meaning and obvious value in beauty and sentiment breathe life into the space. They truly are a room's "objects of desire."

Have you ever admired an arrangement of objects wonderfully displayed on a table in someone's home? If you were to spend some time analyzing why the pieces appeal to you so much, you would probably recognize the arrangement of the objects, as well as the way they relate to each other, is as attractive to you as the individual pieces themselves. This is the art of tablescaping. It is the landscape of grouped pieces that

TABLESCAPING

creates an arrangement that is intriguing and interesting to the onlooker. They can be created throughout the home and not just on tables. Mantles, chests, and desks make wonderful stages for tablescapes. These arrangements can be simple and minimalistic or more cluttered and active. Regardless, the key to achieving a harmonious, interesting tablescape is to pay close attention to the characteristics of the objects related to type, color, texture, and scale. By using one or more common qualities, an eye-catching

tablescape can be successfully developed. Be sensitive to balance and proportion. Symmetrical tablescaping is simpler and works by displaying pairs of items that balance at each end of the display. The more random, asymmetric tablescapes are a bit trickier, but can be very rewarding when executed well. Start with an essential piece—a lamp, a vase, a clock. Build from this piece, one item at a time, with attention to the space between the objects and the way they block and complement each other. Do not line them up in rows as this is only effective with collections of very similar items. Work toward a rhythmic grouping that causes the eye to continually travel over the combined objects. Tablescaping is a trial and error practice. Just like the boutonniere that is perfectly located on a tuxedo's lapel, it takes a number of placements and pinnings of the flower before the eye knows it is just right. So it goes with the arrangement of accessories. Be daring. Try, and try again. Add and subtract. Nothing is set in stone. When it is right, you'll know it.

While tabletop accessories appear countless in their variations, two ways they can be categorized are either ornamental or functional. Ornamental accessories are designed solely for their display value. A ceramic bird or porcelain egg falls into this group. Functional items, on the other hand, are pieces made for a purpose outside of display, yet bring a special, basic quality to a tablescape. Books, bowls, boxes, and candles are wonderful functional pieces employed as tabletop accessories. They bring familiarity and warmth to an arrangement. They help it appear less staged and, in many ways, more relaxed and personal. By stacking or casually intermingling books and boxes within a display, a careless feel is created while, at the same time, various heights and volumes can be developed, contributing to the overall scene. Blending the functional items with the ornamental pieces results in a more dimensional display, both literally and figuratively.

UPPER RIGHT
Often the most challenging to tablescape, this long entry table uses casually placed books, an unhung, framed image, and a repetition of items to cover its surface with a display that appears fresh and spontaneous. The dramatic framed mirror balances the substantial weight of the table.

BOTTOM RIGHT
Simple yet effective, this display complements the bright and eye-catching interest of the sculpture with the weight and texture of the plate and potted dracaena.

The photograph on the right directs the movement of sight. This handsome grouping takes the eye over the tall candlestick lamp, over the ship and writing box, up the topiaried ivy, across the landscape and back to the starting point. It combines a traditional theme and masculine tone into a strong, fluid display. Supported by a magnificent console, this symmetrical setting on the bottom right of the page features two lamps flanking a centered wall image that is eclectically interrupted by dissimilar items placed between the balanced light sources. A sparse composition of natural items on this scroll-top table on the bottom left creates an air of tranquility and mystique.

Nothing in a home tells the story of its inhabitants more than a collection. A single item reflects an interest, while a collection represents a passion. A collection can enrich a room with a quality that comes from what is important to you—what you value and love. The challenge to incorporating a treasured collection in your design scheme is twofold. One is to arrange the items in a way that transforms a hodgepodge into an appealing grouping. The other is to know when enough is enough, to recognize when more becomes less, aesthetically. The art of display is

COLLECTIONS

guided by a sense of proportion and balance, most often achieved through trial and error. There are few fixed rules. However, one rule is that numerous like items have a much better effect visually when grouped rather than scattered throughout a room. It is the difference between a collection of pieces and a cluttering of items. By grouping, the interest of repetition is achieved and the focal point of a collection can be created. The assimilation of like characteristics, whether size, shape, texture, or color, also causes impact.

Collect what you love. Gather it together and show it off. For, just as a pen becomes a tool to sign your signature, a treasured collection is an instrument that personalizes a beautiful room with a style that is truly your own.

All decorating is about memories.
Mrs. Henry Parish

PAGE 64
By displaying the individual pieces of this ceramic collection on stands of varying heights, the grouping becomes animated and interesting.

PAGE 65
Not all collections require careful presentation. Casually gathered in a single place, these rocks and shells create an inviting display.

OPPOSITE
The beauty of this collection is enhanced by hanging the crosses at differing heights. The composition becomes much more interesting than if the pieces were lined up in rows and columns.

UPPER RIGHT
The individual differences in height and shape create the impact as these candlesticks are brought together for comparative interest.

BOTTOM RIGHT
Lending a worn, lived-in look to a room, books have a life beyond the shelf. Here, a collection is loosely stacked, providing visual weight and a sense of relaxed living.

Have you ever thought of your home as a gallery? After all, what is a gallery but a series of rooms with walls? Not unlike your home, right? And just like in a gallery, the walls in your home are the perfect place to exhibit the art you love. Of course, art is much more than painted canvas. Photography, sculptures, tapestries, carvings, and distinctive collections of objects add the perfect character and detail to a home's décor.

When displaying wall décor, a number of lessons can be learned from the gallery experts. First, be sensitive to the wall space around your art. In most cases, art needs room to breathe and should not be crowded on a wall. The impact of the art is increased when given adequate empty wall space as a backdrop. Also, consider the vantage point from which the art will be viewed. Most often, art should be hung at eye level. However, eye level is not always at standing height. Consider how museums hang art lower that is meant to be viewed from a bench set directly across from the piece. If art is viewed opposite a hallway bench, above a buffet seen from a dining chair, or on a nightstand observed from the edge of the bed, eye level is at seating height. If the art or images are small or intricate, it is important to display them at eye level so they can be easily examined and enjoyed. On the other hand, a home with soaring ceilings or spacious

HANGING AROUND

stairwells offers wonderful opportunities to exhibit art high on the walls. The scale of the room and the size of the pieces must be compatible for this to be effective. Larger pieces that can intrigue without needing close-up scrutiny work best in these settings.

Finally, when grouping images or objects, arrange the items to create an identifiable collection and focal point. Keep the space between the items consistent so they do not appear scattered. This will draw the eye into the group and then encourage the examination of each piece. A grouping can be tied together in many ways. A block of color can be painted on the wall behind the collection. The use of frames or matting common to the pieces creates unity. A collective theme in subject matter, technique, or color is effective. Remember, too, that just like a gallery whose exhibits change regularly, so can yours. Be adventurous in displaying images and objects that interest and amuse you. Feel free to move, rearrange, and replace them. While some may find a permanent residence in an ideal location, others welcome movement to continually keep your interior alive and ever changing.

As a detail that decorates a wall, the conventional framed image is just the beginning of a list of endless objects available. Imaginative wall "art" takes on many forms. Look to items that are created for other purposes and consider their impact when mounted on a wall. Elaborately woven rugs, weather-beaten window frames, and raffia-bound dried florals are just the start of this inventive process. If an item strikes you and its color, shape, or story excites you, it may well be the perfect object to accent your walls.

Scale plays a large role in determining the placement and positioning of art on the walls. Large, oversized pieces require a wall with enough surface not only to hold the art, but also to surround it with adequate empty space to eliminate any feeling of crowding or tightness. The capacity of the wall to both house and support the art needs to be generous.

LEFT
The large piece of abstract art is a solo act giving mass and weight to the right-hand wall of this sparsely, yet wonderfully detailed bedroom. In contrast, the two smaller canvases work harmoniously with other accessories on the distressed trunk. The result is a well-designed tablescape that balances well with the neighboring oversized canvas.

As the sun colours flowers so does art colour life.

Sir John Lubbock

Sometimes the most delicious recipes combine traditional ingredients with a pinch of the unexpected. So it is with home décor and detail. An element of surprise, in the form of detail, spices up a room and gives it a unique, personalized flavor. The

SURPRISES

key to making the effect work is contrast and creativity. The detail must deviate from the setting in which it is placed. A jar of colorful antique marbles displayed on a traditional console gives an imaginative touch of whimsy. An African mask hung where you would expect a mirror or framed painting is a novelty. A splash of brilliant color where it wouldn't be anticipated can be provocative. Try enlisting an object or detail outside of the traditional use or setting you would expect to find it. A matted and framed piece of clothing, such as an elegant kimono robe, can add ingenuity and curiosity to a wall. A child's toy or drawing can be amusing and quirky when displayed among more sophisticated accessories. Mechanical and architectural remnants employed as accents and furniture can cause admiring double takes. Set your imagination and sense of humor free. Make room in your home for a surprising twist or two and enjoy the lifted eyebrows and unwitting smiles these unexpected details can cause.

PAGE 72
Frequently, an everyday item can become a strikingly decorative detail when used outside of its original purpose. Here, the opposite has occurred with an unforgettable abstract sculpture serving as a much used entry table in the home.

UPPER RIGHT
A stack of old, colorful suitcases masquerade as a head-turning nightstand in this delightfully quirky bedroom.

UPPER LEFT
A barrage of brilliantly colored product labels cover this chest of drawers, becoming an amusing addition to this kitchen corner.

BOTTOM LEFT
Miniature shopping carts and a barrel drum sink bring a sense of peculiar pageantry to this wonderfully "illustrated" powder room.

OPPOSITE
A discarded fossil from a machine shop becomes the unexpected base of this kitchen's much used center island. The butcher-block top and surrounding concrete counter tops are in keeping with the "no frills" approach to detail in this room.

Your home should be more than a roof over your head or shelter from a storm. It should be a temporary escape from the pressures and pace of daily life. It should give you a sense of yourself, a place that provides an environment that you find spiritually rewarding. If you thrive on tranquillity, the detail in your home should create a peaceful aura. If you enjoy excitement, it should be colorful and interesting at every turn. If you delight in foreign places, your décor should have

SPECIAL PLACES

references and details that take you to your dream destinations, if only in your imagination. Any activity or hobby that cheers you should have a place in your home. After all, cooks have kitchens and artists have studios. The term used to describe the practice of creating a home that we love and spend time in is "nesting." More and more, we choose to nest, spending our free time at home—relaxing, entertaining, and recharging from the demands of everyday life. Sit back and determine what makes you happy when you retreat from the intrusions of the daily grind. Bring this into your home using detail as your tool, and you will create a personal escape.

The golden ochre walls of Rome's Piazza Navonna. The tropical palm leaves of Bali. The muted colors and textures of the desert southwest. These are the nuances of just a few of the faraway places many find irresistible. Because there is a desire to bring the essence of favorite places into our homes, detail is hired to create a sense of place. Natural materials and colors indigenous to a location, identifiable shapes, forms, and decoration that reflect a culture and life-style, all can be integrated into the home as detail. Detail can transport us to what seems continents away, even if we are really just escaping to our homes.

Everybody needs a bit of solitude, a private place to unwind, to meditate and be contentedly alone. From a quiet corner to a peaceful room, detail can create a harmonious setting that encourages reflection and a restful sigh. Consider the many calming details you can bring into your home. Soft, welcoming upholstery, filtering sheers and screens that mellow light, and the flickering flames of candles and fireplaces are just a few. Sight is just one of the senses that contributes. The sound of breeze-swept chimes and the trickle of water from a nearby fountain soothes us. Emotion-evoking aromas like newly cut flowers, freshly baked bread, or hand-milled soaps also add to the experience. Realizing that comfort and peace of mind are key to relaxation, create a place in your home that provides both of these and it will undoubtedly become one of the most valued spaces in your home.

Sometimes it is the smallest details, the finishing touches, that provide the most memorable character to a space. The last-minute throw of a knitted shawl over a sofa arm, a spread of pillows across a bed, or the stacking of books on a table. These are among the wonderful, changeable ways to express a personal style that comes more from the heart than from the head. Even detail can be enriched with detail. Accent pillows can be fringed, collections can be staggered and heightened with stands, wall décor can be hung

FINISHING TOUCHES

with ribbon or iron bars. These are the small creative touches that cause a second look and earn a passing smile. They prove that a space should never be considered "finished." There is always a new way to express yourself through detail. Because your tastes, your likes, and dislikes change through life's experiences, your home should naturally reflect these changes. Traditionalists acquire a taste for contemporary, travelers continually bring home elements of distant utopias. Life changes . . . so should your décor. On a smaller level, the simple changes of the seasons keep a home alive. The holidays and nature's seasonal offerings decorate the home for spurts of time. Unlike a static museum, the home should breathe the essence of living that comes from change. Create a wonderful display of collectibles. Enjoy and admire it until it no longer charms you. Take it apart and start again. Repaint a favorite wall, admire and absorb it. Then repaint it again. Let your home live the life you live—enriched with character and individuality, always open to improvement with something new and interesting.

PAGE 82
Heavily fringed pillows, bold animal prints, leather-bound books, and collections of silver trophies add distinctive pattern, color, and a depth of character to this strongly masculine room.

PAGE 83
The simple and imaginative use of fringed tassels as decorative detail on these carved wooden stools is a wonderful example of a small, yet effective personalized touch in the home.

RIGHT
Layer upon layer of decorative detail brings a unique style and character to this master bedroom. Walls awash in a hand-finished golden ochre and an antique Sumak kilim rug create a stunning background to flourishing detail throughout the room. Kashmere shawls, mix-matched linens, one-of-a-kind pillows, and collected boxes create a memorable room, alive with personality.

SPACE

Defined as the expanse within which all things are contained, space is a valuable commodity in terms of both quantity and quality in the home. Having the room to do what you want and to store your possessions describes a quantitative view of space. The square footage and wall-to-wall expanse of a room is calculated to measure this figure. The qualitative measure of space is a whole other story. It is more abstract, more a matter of having room to breathe or of the feel of openness, balance, and proportion that a room presents. The importance of recognizing the difference between these two is that while a room may not contain the ideal quantity of space, its perceived quality of space can make up for its spatial shortcomings. Detail is the magical tool that can be used to bring quality to spatially challenged rooms.

Detail adds character and personality to a room. It can also flex its muscle in other ways. Detail can actually change the spatial "feel" of a room. Referred to as the illusion of space, it is the way you perceive the size and volume of a room beyond its

ILLUSION OF SPACE

actual dimensions. Obviously, we are not normally fortunate enough to begin with a room that is perfect in size. Some are compact and challenging in their measure. Others can be overly voluminous and uncomfortably large. Detail can change the proportions of the rooms, creating the illusion of a more desirable size in height, width, and depth. For instance, mirrors can seem to miraculously double the size of a room. They bring a sense of added light, air, and volume. Vertical stripes on walls

can add to their height. Dark colors on ceilings lower them. Horizontal details add width to a wall. Beyond surface detail, the placement of furniture and a sensitivity to scale and proportion can expand small spaces and bring a more intimate essence to larger rooms. The goal is to create a room that provides a quality of comfort and ease despite its actual dimensional limitations.

One of the most powerful ways to expand the space of a room is to use mirrors. They can create an illusion of added depth and light to an area that is challenged in both ways. Mirrors are used decoratively in one of two ways. One, they can be attached directly to a surface, like a wall or ceiling. Two, they can be framed and positioned like a piece of art. By placing mirrored glass directly on a wall, it gives an immediate illusion of a room opening up onto itself, dramatically increasing the perception of space. To make a wall disappear by covering it with mirrored glass, it is important that all edges are concealed, running the mirror to the edges of the wall, floor to ceiling. Another space-altering trick is to frame the mirror architecturally, filling a door frame, window frame, or archway with its reflective power. Decorative and framed mirrors can be used on a smaller scale to trick the eye and reflect an image that faces the mirror. Hanging a mirror on a wall opposite a beautiful view or window doubles the opportunity to enjoy the sight. Mirrors also work magic in small, dark corners or halls. They reflect light and depth, seeming to open these dark spaces up.

PAGE 89
An oversized mirror is boldly framed and set near a wall of windows to brighten this small, but seemingly spacious room.

UPPER LEFT
A cozy kitchen is opened up by imagery seen through three window frames filled with mirrored glass. Easily reproduced, the effect of this clever detail on the tight space is almost magical.

BOTTOM LEFT
Reflecting the beauty of this elegant dining room, a magnificently framed mirror enriches the room with the added light it provides.

OPPOSITE
The breathtaking view of this spectacular room is doubled by using floor-to-ceiling mirrors on the wall behind the sofa and carved wooden console. The effective treatment creates the illusion of a marvelous penthouse open on all sides to the vistas beyond.

There are many ways detail can help alter our perception of a room that is spatially challenged. Whether it is small and confining or overly large and vast, the size of a room can seem changed when scale is effectively addressed. Regarding proportion and size, scale refers to the relationship of one object to another as well as to the space in which it is placed. In a large voluminous space, the use of oversized furnishings and large details can make the room seem smaller—more welcoming and comfortable. Also, by creating numerous conversation groupings rather than one large floating arrangement, the area can be brought down to a more human scale. On the other hand, small spaces benefit from details that include dark walls, mirrors, small patterns, and furniture that floats in the room rather than hugging the tight walls.

OPPOSITE
Smartly designed, this small sitting room is big on style. Dark walls expand the modest space giving it depth and a more intimate feel. By covering the upholstery in a rich color that matches the walls, the space is less cut up visually, adding to its roomy appearance. The furnishings are pulled away from the walls and their clean, uncluttered lines as well as the large wall art keep the space simple and orderly.

PAGE 93 UPPER LEFT
Home to a lover of big spaces, this large-scale room is filled appropriately with proportionately ample sofas and a generously sized ottoman. To have used smaller furnishings would have required multiple sitting areas destroying the desired clean, contemporary design.

PAGE 93 BOTTOM LEFT
In this expansive master suite, a handsome glass-topped cocktail table and two sueded accent chairs delineate the sitting area from that of the plush canopy bed, bench, and nightstands. Perfectly scaled for this large room, these elegant furnishings bring an air of sophisticated comfort to the area.

RIGHT
There is something seductively inviting about a chaise lounge. In this living room, a pair of generously proportioned chaises replaces the traditionally used sofa to create a sitting area that is distinctively luxurious. The scale and style of the furnishings, along with muted colors and finishes, interplay perfectly to create a relaxed, yet elegant space.

A focal point is the first thing you notice when you enter a room. It acts as a magnet, immediately drawing your eye to it. A room's primary focal point is normally an architectural feature like a beautifully framed fireplace or an expansive window boasting a breathtaking view. Well-designed rooms regularly have multiple focal points of varying significance. In order of prominence, they draw the eye into the space, give it a point to linger, enjoy, and then send it on to the next. They guide you through a room directing your attention throughout the space and, at the same

FOCAL POINTS

time, distracting it from settling on any shortcomings or blemishes the room may have. When you create focal points, start with the most obvious. If the room's natural "attention grabber" is desirable, like a wonderful pair of French doors or a magnificent mantle, enhance this focal point with detail. Add color, lighting, or accessorization. If your eye is intuitively drawn to a less desirable object, downplay the item by blending it into the space and creating a stronger "point of view" that steals your attention away from it. As you create additional focal points to give the room a sense of movement, remember that these secondary points need to have a lesser impact so they don't compete with the primary eye-catcher. They may include a collection of treasured objects, a brilliant piece of wall décor, a vase overflowing with vibrant flowers, or a treasured antique chest or armoire. Depending on the size and nature of the room, three significant focal points are enough. If you find that your eye doesn't know where to rest or is jumping all around the room without finding a natural resting place, you have most likely created too many points of interest or have given them similar weight in terms of attraction. Start with your main point of interest and slowly add the others with decreasing degrees of magnetism. The result will be a well-choreographed room that delights the eye as it dances throughout the space.

PAGE 96
A disciplined restraint of detail and competing focal points pays tribute to this spectacular coastal view. It beckons the eye into the room and only after its initial magnetism ebbs, do we then admire the secondary focal point, the abstract image above the fireplace.

OPPOSITE
Some rooms come equipped with architectural focal points. Others, like this smartly detailed dining area, do not. Originally unexceptional, the back wall became a stunning focal point with the creative addition of not only a brilliantly colored abstract painting, but also a painted plane of acid green that intensifies and enlarges this primary focal point.

UPPER RIGHT
Color is perhaps the strongest way to create a focal point. In this muted, contemporary living room, a startling red image on a distant wall successfully catches the eye and immediately draws it back into the billiard room.

BOTTOM RIGHT
A small space bursting with detail, this stairway uses a number of effects to draw the visitor down-stairs. The image of the blue vase on the three-legged table is the prominent focal point. A mirror exaggerates the vase's attention-getting power while, at the same time, reflects a silver urn that can only be seen in whole by descending the stairs. The stair-stepped painted wall and scattered colored tiles also arouse interest and movement.

Editing can be therapeutic for both you and your home. It provides a sense of freedom from the excess and clutter that life lures into your living space. While some people prefer sparse, simpler décor, others like collections and objects, surrounding them at every turn. Both directions benefit from editing. It weeds out the meaningless surplus so that the things you love are given more attention and power in display. The mental exercise of removing everything from the room and replacing only the items that are important and meaningful to you is a great way to start the editing process. You will be

EDIT

amazed at the insignificant bric-a-brac and odd pieces that suffocate the pieces that you cherish. The adage that too much of a good thing is bad holds true for detail. For detail to be effective, it can't be weighted down or congested with trivial excess. Actually, editing is like gardening. If you weed out the nonnecessities, prune and trim the details, leaving only the things that you love, you will have a home that breathes easier and blooms with clarity and character. So forge ahead, edit your décor and you will find you enjoy the detail you treasure even more than before.

A *discerning eye needs only a hint, and under-statement leaves the imagination free to build its own elaborations.*

Russell Page

PAGE 100
Sometimes the best way to edit a space is to strip it down to the bare essentials. Then add a detail or two that stirs your emotions. Here, a bed and bedside table are necessities. The plush down bedding, sunny flowers, fresh apples, and flickering candle finish the space with a simple, contented ambiance.

UPPER RIGHT
The clearly edited, yet approachable space of this sparsely decorated room boasts a repetition of linear forms. The window, patterned rug, and unadorned furnishings reflect the owner's uncluttered approach to life.

BOTTOM RIGHT
When the architectural detail in a home is so profoundly beautiful, it is criminal to distract from it with excess. Here, elongated candlesticks and a simple carving on the wall welcome without drawing attention away from the beams, fluid plastered walls, and impressive flagstone floors.

OPPOSITE
To effectively use minimal detail in a space requires an even greater attention to the qualities that add character to the room. Here, a keen use of lighting, sculpture, and color make the sparse design of this entry aesthetically striking.

OUTDOORS

Acting as host to some of life's simplest pleasures, a home's gardens can intoxicate with their peaceful, relaxing ambiance. Slow dinners on soft summer nights, unplanned naps beneath tree-filtered sunlight, and contemplative moments in intimate garden spaces, all savored under forever changing skies. When properly created, gardens are an extension of the architecture and character of the home. They are the result of inspired minds, personal style, and an abundance of nature's wonders enriched with imaginative details. From the simplest hand-painted tile to the most elaborate gazebo, outdoor detail breathes life into uninspired gardens just as it does to the most basic interior spaces. Here, among the flowering roses and chirping birds, detail instills a quality of individual taste and character that begins inside the home, flows through the doors and resonates throughout the landscape.

Reflecting upon the design of a home most often leads us to imagine the indoor spaces created by walls, ceilings, and floors. However, today's home designs and life-styles blur the line that delineates the "in" and the "out." Expansive windows and double doors beckon the outside in and those of us on the inside, out. The garden and yard have become an integral part of today's home. Whether it is under a roof

OUTSIDE ROOMS

or under the outstretched branches of a treasured shade tree, outdoor living areas have become as much as a part of the home as the classic family room. These welcoming spaces—the patio, the porch, the terrace, the deck, and the private gardens—offer the opportunity to extend the personality of our interiors to the outside. Our personal style can be reflected by the way we design them. Just as with the inside décor, the creative use of details can bring a unique character and finishing touch that amuses and delights those who experience these outdoor "living" rooms.

PAGES 106–107
This outdoor room's sense of comfort is created by introducing details more traditionally enjoyed indoors. Freshly cut flowers, flickering candles, linens, and framed art work hand-in-hand with garden-style accents of hanging rakes and transplanted window frames. The combination creates a welcoming room in which to read, relax, and entertain, well into the evening.

LEFT
An isolated woven-leather chair invites solitude and quiet reading in this secluded patio. Scattered earthen jugs, a tiger-striped pillow, and the tropical leaves of a thriving split-leaf philodendron bring the sense of a jungle clearing to this contemplative space.

OPPOSITE
The sight and sound of this carved stone fountain becomes the focus of this private outdoor space. Symmetrically placed lanterns, candle-sticks, and arm chairs suggest a quiet visit with a friend while enjoying the play of light filtering through overhead beams.

A sanctuary in the middle of the garden, a gazebo provides both shelter from summer showers as well as an intimate retreat to languish in the fragrance, sights, and sounds of the surrounding landscape. Like the songs of the sirens, arbors tempt and lure us to pass beneath their vine-covered frames. Pergolas, too, support overhead twists of climbing foliage

STRUCTURES

as they create a magical passageway seductively leading us to the mysteries of unknown gardens beyond. Who can see a garden bridge without passing over it simply to experience the crossing? These are just a few of the stylish structures that lend character and personality to a home's landscape. Functionally, they provide a focal point that catches the eye. They become a destination within the garden. Many offer shade and shelter while supporting rambling vines and tendrils. As a transition between sections of the garden, structures can physically direct the experience of exploration, leading from open lawns to secret gardens. Foremost, they are large-scale detail successfully helping to establish the overall mood and style of the garden.

Bridges are like a man-made rainbow rising from a garden. They arch out of the ground, creating a point of interest while traversing reflective waters, a dry ravine, or indentation in the property. While some give easy access to an otherwise un-reachable part of the garden, many are created solely for their visual charm and are not designed for crossing. In either case, bridges have an undeniable magnetism that requires us to investigate their setting and purpose in the garden.

UPPER RIGHT
Spanning a quiet lily pond, this arched wooden bridge transports from a beauganvilla-lined garden to a small green aviary across the tranquil water. The setting offers an enchanting destination in this wonderfully detailed yard.

The gazebo, designed for "gazing out," was originally styled as a small building placed within a rambling landscape giving it structure and a haven for lovers of the garden. Today, gazebos are still the stars of many beautifully fashioned yards and have remained stylish retreats where hours of sheltered relaxation can be enjoyed.

BOTTOM RIGHT
Furnished with interior benches, this wonder-fully designed gazebo offers an enclosed sanctuary that provides a place to become one with the garden while being sheltered from inclement weather. It is half-hidden in a distant corner of a lavish garden, creating both a teasing focal point and irresistible detail that lures all visitors to the outer edges of this property.

Arbors are magical in the experience they provide for wanderers of a garden. Rising above the lush plantings with a coat of flowering roses or twisting vines, arbors lure the willing explorer to pass beneath their framework simply to learn what lies on the other side. Popular as far back as the eighteenth century, these structures have become a wonderful spectacle in the gardens of today. They are easily designed, placed, and planted, giving them status as a favorite focal point for avid gardeners as well as lackeys who simply enjoy a beautiful yard. They are built from a variety of materials in a spectacular range of forms. They are wonderful at providing dramatic transition from one area of the garden to another, and are sometimes built with attached benches, tempting visitors to sit and luxuriate under the filtered sun of their foliage-woven frames.

LEFT
Alive with the sweet smell of climbing roses, this elaborate wooden arbor performs an alluring entry to the flagstone patio beyond. The built-in bench offers a much used retreat to sit, read the mail, and enjoy the garden leading to this wonderful setting.

Perhaps the most memorable feature of a landscape is water. Water evokes emotion as it hypnotizes with its sights and sounds. Visually, it is alluring in its fluid movement, sparkling cascades, and still reflections of the surrounding landscape. The sky dances on its surface as we unwittingly lose time gazing into its depths and mirrored images from above. From the smallest

WATER

pond or rippling stream to a formal pool or tiered fountain, well-designed water features can entice and enrapture as they become irresistible focal points and destinations within the landscape. Water offers an assortment of sounds with which to add audible detail to the garden. It serenades with the trickle of a fountain, burble of a brook, gurgle of a waterfall, and the splash of a swimming pool. All of this is like music to the ear while, at the same time, water obscures undesirable noise unnatural to the garden setting. From pools to fountains, water features are wonderful details that are, to many, the most effective way to bring character, movement, and refreshing breath to gardens of the home.

While many water features are magnificent spectacles that stand out from the surrounding landscape, others derive their charm from blending into the gardens and nature that encompass them. No longer must fish ponds, swimming pools, and bubbling hottubs stand out as contrasting accents to the garden's theme. Building with indigenous materials and planting in a natural style results in water features that appear as if they existed long before the landscape was tamed.

PAGE 113
Lush gardens and thriving water iris create a secluded spot for this shadowed lily pond. Its setting is so subtle that often the only way it is discovered is by the sound of trickling water pouring from the tilted urn of the bronze figure.

LEFT
As a starry night settles on the desert, this magnificently designed landscape becomes one with its setting. The hot-tub and swimming pool are disguised with native rock and blend into the vista beautifully. The rounded fireplace removes the chill from the open sky, warming a wonderful outdoor dining area.

OPPOSITE
Like an oasis in the middle of the Sonoran desert, this beautiful swimming pool seems as natural to the setting as the boulders and mesquite trees that surround it. A man-made stream flows effortlessly into the pool. Its water's origin appears to be somewhere in the distance, but is actually not far away as it is fueled by a pump that draws water from the destined pool.

Fountains are one of the easiest and most decorative ways to bring the enchanting nature of water to the garden. Whether in an intimate courtyard, a walled entrance, or an open backyard, fountains effortlessly offer the captivating sound of trickling water while creating a visual point of interest to the space. They come in infinite forms, styles, sizes, and shapes. From the trickle of water into an open urn to the spectacle of cascading water falling from the tiers of a stone sculpture, fountains provide a way to display your personal style while incorporating the magic of water into your garden.

OPPOSITE
A pack of carved dogs perform duel roles as they support the bowls of this handsome cantera stone fountain while spouting water into its broad basin. This unique water feature wonderfully accents this courtyard surrounded by adobe walls and red tile roofs.

UPPER RIGHT
This uniquely carved stone fountain tames the wildflower garden in which it is placed. Its small stature and easy burbling sound make it perfectly scaled, in both sight and sound, for this understated setting.

BOTTOM RIGHT
Verdigris mermaids support a water-filled shell above a tranquil, open basin. The fountain is a character-filled focal point for the blooming garden that surrounds it.

LEFT
Water-spewing elephants, aligning a stair-stepped wall, splash into an indigo tiled trough. The echo of the water charms the distant dining area that is detailed with assorted pillows and a large ship's lantern.

OPPOSITE UPPER LEFT
A number of water-spurting frogs sit above flowing canals of water spouts, paying homage to the wonderful effect fountains make on a landscape.

OPPOSITE UPPER RIGHT
Rising from the depths of a rectangular pool, stacked-stone pillars gush forth water from their wide-mouthed troughs. They take this rather ordinary pool and make it extraordinary in both style and sound.

OPPOSITE BOTTOM RIGHT AND BOTTOM LEFT
Timelessly captured in a stuccoed wall, Bacchus, in the company of his muses, spouts water into the far end of an imaginatively detailed swimming pool. The ingenious landscape of tumbled pillars complements the Pompeian-like theme of the garden.

Like accessories inside the home, garden ornaments are a great way to place your signature upon the landscape outdoors. Garden ornaments lure us into the yard, encouraging us to explore in hopes of finding more. Likely undiscovered in a stationary view or casual glance, the unexpectedly discovered first ornament hints at others and piques the curiosity of the now charmed wanderer. Ornaments flavor with humor, mystery, and wonder. From a tin-roofed birdhouse perched in a tree to a stone sphere nestled in creeping ground cover, ornaments become integral in the garden as a series of focal points that guide us through the space. They set the pace as we stop and admire

ORNAMENTS

before continuing on the journey. Prominently displayed objects, seen from a distance, can be used as strong focal points drawing us into the farthest corners of the landscape. Sculptures, statues, and ancient sundials are conspicuous visuals that boldly adorn the garden while enhancing it with a distinctive style. In selecting ornaments for your garden, no object should be overlooked. If it has special meaning to you, does not overwhelm the rest of the space, and adds a touch of whimsy, surprise, or mystery to your outdoor "living" room, it is a detail that deserves a special place in your garden.

Defining garden ornamentation is simple . . . it is whatever you want it to be. Any object that brings you pleasure, that you place in your landscape, is your personal definition. Certainly, the items most often pictured when discussing garden ornaments and accessories would include statuary, birdbaths and bird-houses, stone urns, and fountains. But what about the plastic pink flamingo? It is just the beginning of the endless unique objects that can bring your personal style into the garden. Other ideas? Gazing globes reflecting the summer's flowers, or twig baskets waiting to be filled with fresh vegetables from the yard. Watering cans, terra-cotta pots, and rusted wheelbarrows potted with brilliant geraniums. The possi-bilities go on and on. Be bold in your choices and careful in their placement. Just as with the details you bring to the interior of your home, outdoor ornaments have the power to either enhance a landscape or blemish it. Introduce it to the garden and determine how it fits and relates to the setting. If it does not, try it elsewhere. The same object that can mar one scene can enrich another.

PAGE 124
Early morning sprinklers shower a solitary figure of a child standing among sky-reaching hollyhocks. Sculpted statues like this have brought delight to gardens for centuries, acting as permanent friends that are at home outdoors.

PAGE 125
Befriended by a whimsical copper dragonfly and ball-centered flower, this miniature red gazing globe reflects the beauty of the surrounding garden. Normally much larger and available in many colors, these mirrored spheres are popular, fanciful ornaments. They attract the eye with the brilliance of the skies above and the beauty of the surrounding landscape with every glance.

UPPER LEFT
Casually placed on an age-old stump, this armillary sphere represents an ornament that has found its home in gardens for ages. The armillary is a centuries-old astronomical instrument, based on a theory that placed the earth at the center of the universe. Here, it is company to wildflowers and untamed brush. More often, it is effectively used as a focal point when located on a stone base in the open yard.

BOTTOM LEFT
There are few places to spend time that are more pleasurable than a garden. So it is fitting that one of the oldest and most favored garden ornaments is one designed to measure this well-spent time. Sundials bring classic style to a garden and should be placed in a sunny open spot. This dial is decorated with the zodiac, while others feature phrases, heavenly figures, and other artistic ornamentation.

A clock the time may wrongly tell;
I, never, if the sun shine well.

Anonymous

PAGE 127
A series of garden spaces is presented like chapters in a book. Each telling a story with ornamentation that must be experienced before moving on to the next. The figure overlooking the small pond makes a wonderful respite on the way to viewing, up-close, the alluring armillary beyond. A marvelous example of effectively placed outdoor focal points.

UPPER RIGHT
Birds bring life and entertainment to a garden. There are many ornaments that lure them into the home's landscape and lend personality to the yard. Birdbaths, birdhouses, and feeders are the most popular. All are wonderful ways to help make your garden home to these winged friends.

BOTTOM RIGHT
Telling the daily tale of temperature, this easy-to-read outdoor thermometer is perfectly mounted on a tree just outside the kitchen window.

If it can be filled with soil and hold up to outdoor elements, chances are it can be used as a container in some creatively detailed garden. Among the more traditional containers—pots, urns, and planting boxes—there is such a diversity in style that these offer wonderful opportunities to direct the sense of style desired within a garden. The warmth and earthiness of terracotta works where the stately elegance of a fluted stone urn doesn't. So it is with a weathered wooden window box spilling with geraniums in contrast to a mosaic-covered pot planted with cacti. Of course, the unexpected can also bring charm to the garden. Old tin watering cans, wooden wheelbarrows, painted stoneware, copper troughs, and woven baskets are filled with soil and brilliantly colored flowers. Here again, a sense of surprise that complements its surroundings is the goal. If it is jarring or distracts from the essence of the garden, its inclusion should be rethought.

As an outdoor detail, seating is primary. Whether it takes the shape of a bench, chair, or rock, outdoor seating offers both function and form to a garden or landscape. Functionally, seating provides a respite, a place to sit and enjoy the views, smells, and sounds the garden proffers. Seating acts like the conductor of a musical. It orchestrates

OUTDOOR SEATING

the exploration of the landscape by providing the pace of how one takes in the outdoor theatre. A well-placed seat suggests a pause before continuing. A bench may be placed before passing under an arbor to propose that one enjoys this portion of the garden

before passing into another. The lack of seating actually encourages one to continue the journey in anticipation of what may lie ahead. Seating also directs the view. It suggests the sights and vistas to be observed. It may overlook a broad landscape or, on the other hand, offer a view of a garden or ornament. Seating suggests the social manner in which to experience the garden. Multiple wicker chairs under outstretched oak branches invite a gathering of friends and family. Picnic table benches and patio chairs accommodate outdoor barbecues and alfresco dining. A flat rock by a running waterfall, on the other hand, provides a solitary place for quiet meditation. To determine the placement for seating on a functional level, one should wander throughout the landscape or gardens and find those places where it feels natural to stop and enjoy the property. The view of the house, the overlook of the landscape, the shade of a tree, or the fragrance of a garden often hint at seating placement.

In form, seating becomes an aesthetic accent for the outdoors and can be very useful in creating a focal point in a landscape. A conspicuously placed group of chairs at the end of a tree row or a white bench circling the trunk of an aged tree immediately draws our eyes to this accessory of the landscape. On the other hand, often the design calls for less. When nestled beneath a climbing rose or among a well-tended garden's blooms, a bench becomes less prominent and is secondary to its surroundings. When determining the type of seating to be used, one can look beyond the obvious bench or chair. Quite often a low garden wall, the railing of a deck or a large nonconspicuously placed boulder can offer a place to sit and relax.

RIGHT
The stone bench gives a garden weight and a sense of permanence. It seems rooted to the earth and as permanent as the full-grown oak. Along a wandering path, it invites a place to rest that is almost irresistible. Beside this pebble-strewn trail, this carved stone bench is tucked into the bushes, being decorative without being obtrusive.

OPPOSITE
This handsome teak bench is paired with a potted, stone urn to give a sense of simple elegance to this curving brick path. Planted at the foot of the bench, blooming alyssum envelopes all who sit here with its sweet fragrance.

Seating not only provides a place to sit but also helps define the style of the garden. White wicker relates beautifully to seaside settings while ornate wrought iron accommodates a more formally styled landscape. Carved stone benches are classic in use and wooden Adirondack chairs are perfect for the ease and comfort of casual, open yards. A hammock, even when left empty, presents thoughts of lazy summer days spent counting clouds. These images all represent details that mutely, yet dramatically, participate in a garden's unique style.

OPPOSITE
A stunning transition from the house to the garden, this elaborately framed bench allows its visitors to be bathed in dappled sunlight filtering through climbing roses and overhead beams. The style and scale of the piece is perfect for the casual elegance of the large open area and, as a focal point in the garden, is flawless.

UPPER AND BOTTOM LEFT
To settle in the backward pitch of a weathered Adirondack chair on a warm summer's day is heaven. To view one offering a cold lemonade from across the yard is irresistible. Both promise the unhurried relaxation what the season is all about.

When all is said and done, creating a home that is truly yours and expresses who you are is like preparing a favorite recipe. Once the basic ingredients are gathered and mixed, the unique flavor results from the special spices and flavorings you select, measure and add at your discretion. The finished dish truly reflects your personal taste. So it is with a home transformed with detail. By choosing and adding elements that are special to you and tell a story of your taste, style, and personality, the rooms and gardens speak of you. The spaces come alive with a unique character that is yours alone.

If you have an appetite for style and a desire to create a welcoming and inspiring home, brimming over with self expression, detail is the secret ingredient. It can season a room and garden, turning a home from ordinary to extrordinary!

Brad Mee, creative director for a custom fashion house, has worked in the fields of interior and fashion design, advertising, and home furnishings. His work has been published in home and garden publications. In addition to his work in the fashion industry, Brad provides design services for personal clients, helping them to bring the detail and character to their homes that he writes about in *Design Is in the Details*.

Brad resides in Phoenix, Arizona, where he lives in and has taken part in restoring a historic Mediterranean-style home, featured throughout *Design Is in the Details*.

ACKNOWLEDGMENTS

To the talented photographers who contributed the images from creative designers, proud homeowners, and skilled builders, I am thankful. To the designers and manufacturers who favored us with their work and to my friends at Chapelle, I am grateful.

In particular, a special thank you goes to Dino Tonn for his substantial contributions to this book. His photography brilliantly showcases his talent and broad range of projects.

DINO TONN PHOTOGRAPHY
5433 EAST KATHLEEN ROAD
PHOENIX, ARIZONA 85254
(602) 765-0455
An attention to detail and true artistry in lighting have made Dino Tonn one of the leading architectural photographers in the Southwest. Specializing in award winning architectural and golf course photography, Tonn has been photographing much of the Southwest's finest architecture for the past 11 years. He serves clients in the hospitality field as well as architects, interior designers, developers, and many other design- related businesses and publications. His work has been featured in regional and national publications. Tonn is a native of Arizona and resides with his wife and two children in Scottsdale, Arizona.

KIM CORNELISON
PHOTOGRAPHER AND PHOTO STYLIST
3150 VALLEY RIDGE COURT
WEST DES MOINES, IOWA 50265
(515) 554-8146
A specialist in home and garden photography for editorial and commercial clients, her photography appears in leading national and regional Home and Garden publications.

DAVID MICHAEL MILLER ASSOCIATES
7034 EAST FIRST AVENUE
SCOTTSDALE, ARIZONA 85251
(480) 425-7545
A custom interior design studio committed to creating unique and beautiful environments for its clients.

PATRICK LEE DESIGN
3911 FIFTH AVENUE SUITE 212
SAN DIEGO, CALIFORNIA 92103
(619) 294-3370
A member of A.S.I.D., Patrick Lee has been serving residential, corporate, contract, and hospitality clients throughout the country for over 20 years. In addition to interior design services, he also provides furniture design to his clients. His work has been featured in national and regional publications including *Architectural Digest*.

GLENN CORMIER PHOTOGRAPHY
3940 7TH AVENUE   SUITE 117
SAN DIEGO, CALIFORNIA 92103
(619) 297-5151
Glenn Cormier is an award-winning photographer who produces a variety of commercial and fine-art work, with an emphasis on architecture and interior design.

KREISS ENTERPRISES
8525 CAMINO SANTA FE
SAN DIEGO, CALIFORNIA 92121
1-800-KREISS1
Featuring a trademark of casual comfort, Kreiss boasts a unique look of elegance for the home. The Kreiss Collection features an international mix of custom handmade furniture, unique accessories, professional design consulting, exclusive fabrics, and luxury bed linens. Showrooms nationwide and Saudi Arabia.

CENTURY FURNITURE
P.O. BOX 608
HICKORY, NORTH CAROLINA 28603
(828) 328-1851
Source of fine wood and upholstered home furnishings for the discriminating homeowner. Century Furniture available through fine home furnishing retailers nationwide.

CREDITS

Designers & Photography

Cindy Antich 51, 57(br)

Arnett-Romero 42

Patty Biller 81

Eric Bron 90(ul)

Ccbg Architects 12, 45

Casa Del Encanto 20(br)

Century Furniture 62(ur), 62(br), 63(ur), 63(br), 63(bl), 86, 144

Sandy Cozens 49, 83

Rick Daugherty 38(br), 75

Edmundson Design 104–105

Est. Est. 25(bl)

Fannin Interiors 71, 98, 99(br)

Gaye Ferrara 25(ul), 50(ur)

Jan Friedman 6(ul), 50(bl)

Trent Gasbarra 15(ul), 57(ur)

Ward Harris 36, 48, 52, 73, 74(ur)

Bess Jones 66

Eddie Jones 21

Kreiss Enterprises 16–17, 33, 90(bl), 91, 93(bl), 94–95

Patrick Lee 92, 96, 97, 103

Brad Mee 13, 14, 15, 24, 85, 138–139

David Michael Miller 2, 8, 10, 28, 34–35, 39, 50(br), 60, 67(br), 89

Jeff Page 44

Pela 74(ul)

Powers Interiors 59

Gordon Rogers 32

Rondo Pools 38(ur), 116

Billi Springer Design 5

Wiseman & Gale 20(bl), 30(l)

Photographers

Glenn Cormier 92, 96, 97, 103

Kim Cornelison
7(l), 7(ctr), 15(bl), 20(ur), 22, 31(r), 37(bl), 40, 41, 43, 58, 61, 65, 67(ur), 69, 70(ul), 70(br), 80(ul), 80(bl), 88, 100, 102(br), 108, 109, 112(ur), 114, 115, 117, 119(ur), 119(br), 121(bl), 121(ur), 121(br), 125, 130, 135, 142

Leslie M. Newman 110, 111, 112(bl), 126(ul), 131(ul) (bl) (br), 132

Robert Perron 2, 54–55, 106, 113, 127, 133, 136

Dino Tonn
2, 3, 5, 6(l), 6(r), 7(r), 8, 10, 12, 13, 14, 15(ul), 15(ur), 18, 19, 20(bl), 20(br), 21, 23, 24, 25(ul), 25(bl), 26, 27, 28, 29, 30(l), 32, 34–35, 36, 37(ul), 37(ur), 37(br), 38(br), 39, 42, 44, 45, 46–47, 48, 49, 50(ur), 50(bl), 50(br), 51, 52, 53, 56, 57(ur), 57(br), 59, 60, 66, 67(br), 70(bl), 71, 72, 73, 74(ul), 74(bl), 74(ur), 75, 78, 79, 81, 83, 84–85, 89, 90(ul), 93(ul), 98, 99(ur), 99(br), 104–105, 116, 118, 120, 121(ul), 138–139

Scot Zimmerman 80(br)

The publisher would like to thank those additional designers and photographers who are not identified on these lists but whose work is featured throughout these pages.

Photodisks

Artiville, LLC Images (© 1997)
64–65

Corbis Corporation Images (© 1999,
2000) 1, 76, 106–107, 128(ur) (br),
136(br)

Photodisc, Inc. Images (© 2000) 30,
77, 86, 101, 102, 122, 123, 124, 126,
129, 136(bl)

INDEX

God is in the Details.

Mies van de Rohe